I0076669

GET PAID TO SHOP

BECOME A
MYSTERY SHOPPER

e. b. williams

Published by LauraSuchan.com

GET PAID TO SHOP: GUIDE TO MYSTERY SHOPPING

Copyright © 2016 by E. B. Williams

All rights reserved. In accordance with the U. S. Copyright Act of 1976, the scanning, uploading, and electronic sharing of any part of this book without the permission of the publisher constitute unlawful piracy and theft of the author's intellectual property. If you would like to use material from the book (other than for review purposes), prior written permission must be obtained by contacting the publisher.

Thank you for your support of the author's rights.

Published in Canada by Laura Suchan (laurasuchan.com).

First Edition: August 2016

ISBN 978-0-9916799-2-8

GET PAID TO SHOP: GUIDE TO MYSTERY SHOPPING

What is it?

All of us do it. Some of us are fast and some are slow. Some days you'll do it indoors, other days outside. Sometimes you do it in the morning, sometimes at night.

It can be done in your own neighbourhood, at malls or department stores, on cruise ships, at theme parks and travel agencies, in other cities and towns, and even in other countries. Actually, it can be done almost anywhere, any day of the week and any time of day!

You can do it alone or with a friend, with your spouse, your children or your neighbours. Sometimes you'll want to spend the whole day doing it.

What is it?

It's shopping.

Shopping is a wonderful experience. There's nothing to worry about. There's no rush. Just relax, and enjoy where you are. Window-shop as you saunter down the street. Go in the store and try on a few outfits, spinning slowly and admiring yourself in the mirror.

Take a break for lunch and then continue with the rest of the day. Visit fashion stores, home decorating stores, mobile phone kiosks, hairdressing salons and more. Enjoy a day filled with pleasant and enjoyable shopping experiences.

Not too many other activities offer the sheer pleasure and rewards that shopping has to offer.

Where else can you wander through climate-controlled, beautifully decorated walkways of marble floors, with sparkling chandeliers overhead and the sounds of sweet music echoing lightly in the background?

Exquisitely decorated areas are everywhere your eye roams. Perfectly trimmed plants and colourful flowers give a hint of ambrosial aromatic pleasure. Friendly salespeople are available to grant your every wish. They are your guides on this journey, to advise you and help you. Follow them, listen to them, ask their advice.

Modern day malls and department stores are the next best thing to paradise. And literally hundreds of stores in your area are available every day of the week for your total shopping enjoyment.

jobslinger.com. I ask for bonuses and am willing to travel regularly within a hundred miles one way."

<u>Author's Note:</u>

This is not a typical mystery shopper.

The typical mystery shopper does three or four shops a week and earns $300 to $400 a month for those shops.

However, if you can search them out and wish to do several shops each day, it is quite possible to earn the level of income that the article talks about.

One nice thing about mystery shopping is that you can work as little or as much as you want to. You can do one shop a month, or six in a single day. You can arrange your job schedule as best suits your own lifestyle.

GET PAID TO SHOP: GUIDE TO MYSTERY SHOPPING

Until now, you might have thought that spending a day shopping would mean spending lots of your hard-earned money. On the contrary, I'm here to show you a new way to discover all the benefits that malls, department stores and retail outlets can offer you without spending any of your own money! There is a way for someone else to pay for your meal, your haircut, your oil change or car repair, your gasoline purchase, your gift cards!

What is this wonderful new way to shop?

It's called "mystery shopping."

This book is designed to guide you through the process of applying to a mystery shopping company, applying for and accepting assignments, and completing your assignments efficiently in order to complete the required documentation and collect your fees.

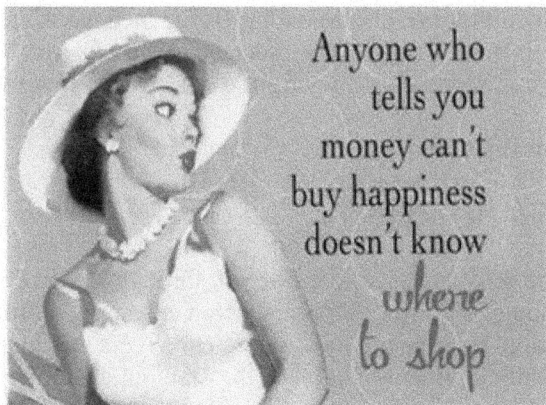

Anyone who tells you money can't buy happiness doesn't know *where to shop*

In Conclusion

Thank you for your interest in becoming a "Mystery Shopper". By implementing the systems and contacting the Businesses in this manual, you can now start making some fantastic money as a "Mystery Shopper". You will have a wonderful new lifestyle shopping at magnificent malls, beautiful department stores, designer clothing shops, specialty stores and hundreds more! And the amazing part is... you <u>Get Paid to Shop</u> plus you get <u>Free Merchandise</u>! The opportunities that Mystery Shopping offers are truly unlimited!

Mystery Shopping truly is the ultimate dream job! Now that you have read this entire manual and are fully prepared to be a Mystery Shopper, I urge you to start right away. There's no better time to make money than today!

Have a great life!

e.b. williams
author

TABLE OF CONTENTS

The biggest lie I tell
myself is
"I don't need
to write that down,
I'll remember it."

GET PAID TO SHOP: GUIDE TO MYSTERY SHOPPING
Chapter One:

The Story Behind "Mystery Shopping"

Do you have fond memories of taking a road trip across the country on vacation, or even across a single large city? Something that you probably noticed as you drove for miles and miles are the unmistakable McDonald's Golden Arches. It seems no matter where you are, you can always find them! You could be in one of the smallest towns in the country, or in a zoo, or even at a baseball stadium, and you will probably come across those famous Golden Arches, and see Ronald McDonald inviting you into the restaurant. With more than 10,000 locations in the United States alone, it's easy to see why you're going to notice a McDonald's restaurant in nearly every town, city, or suburb.

I am also sure at some time during your travels you have stopped at a McDonald's to get something to eat. You know that every McDonald's will have that Quarter-Pounder, French fries and soft drink combo that you've been thinking about all afternoon. It's guaranteed. You also know that when you enter, it will be only a matter of a few minutes to get your meal. The atmosphere will be casual, the washrooms will be clean, and the chairs will be comfortable.

The reason that you made that final decision to stop at McDonald's is simply that you knew what to expect. You can always count on the food, service and atmosphere to be the same. You can find your meal cooked exactly the same, in every part of the country. That is certainly not easy to come by. The only way that happens is if the restaurant chain sends a representative from McDonald's Corporate Headquarters to each and every one of these locations every single day to make sure that the cooks prepare each meal in the exact same manner.

How does the food turn out almost exactly the same in each location?

The answer is really quite simple. Stores and restaurants that have many or even thousands of different locations rely on Mystery Shoppers all over the country, to check every location. By assigning an ordinary customer go to each store and report back to the corporate offices on the service, cleanliness and food quality, they can guarantee the same consistent excellence at every store.

Mystery Shoppers provide a very valuable information source for any Corporate Headquarters about their stores.

GET PAID TO SHOP: GUIDE TO MYSTERY SHOPPING

Since the Mystery Shoppers are working 'undercover', the salespeople at the store will treat them like normal customers. In this way, Mystery Shoppers can provide an unbiased assessment of their shopping experience. Their report will be used by management to help to improve the quality of their service throughout the chain. You, as a "Mystery Shopper", will be providing this valuable information and you will get paid very well for it!

Thousands of stores use Mystery Shoppers. Mystery Shoppers are used in department stores, clothing stores, electronic and video stores, fast-food establishments, banks, auto service and repair shops, and hardware stores. Any retailers that consider their customer service a vital component of their financial success are likely to contact a firm that provides the services of Mystery Shoppers in order to verify the quality of their customer service.

Mystery Shoppers help to provide a communication link between a Corporate Headquarters and all of their stores. In this way, without going to each location, Corporate can find out precisely how clean the stores are, how effective their service is, and how well customers are treated. Big companies with many locations across the country can rely on Mystery Shoppers to go and visit each of their locations.

GET PAID TO SHOP: GUIDE TO MYSTERY SHOPPING

In all companies, the customers are the most important decision makers. By describing their experiences at a store in as much detail as possible, Mystery Shoppers give Corporate, who may be located thousands of miles away, a much clearer picture of the operation of that store. Without Mystery Shoppers, corporate headquarters would never get a real perspective on what goes on at each store on a regular basis. With Mystery Shoppers, they can now implement systems to make sure that each of their stores are operated consistently to ensure maximum customer satisfaction.

The corporate headquarters and management of a big company have many responsibilities of their own, as you can imagine. They don't have time to keep track of what's happening at each of their stores. If an owner does have the opportunity to travel to any of his stores for a quick inspection, you can be sure that all of the employees are well aware of his impending arrival. They may spend days preparing for his inspection. They may work overtime cleaning the entire store getting it in the best condition. When the big day arrives and the owner walks through the front door, every employee will surely be on his or her best behaviour.

What happens when you or I, the average customer, walks through the door? Is the store tidy and clean? Are the employees on their best behaviour? Is customer satisfaction a priority? As you can see there's a tremendous need for Mystery Shoppers. They are there to report on how a <u>normal</u> customer gets treated, in an everyday situation.

Mystery Shoppers are not hired to spy on employees or stores. They do not inspect every detail, look for things to correct or go out of their way to find problems. They take into account procedures and events as they are and later, they write a brief summation of what happened during their assigned shopping trip.

After the management of the store reads these summaries, the management will know what is REALLY going on at the stores. Managers will gain an insight into how the average customers feel when they shop and also how they are treated. Mystery Shoppers are a vital, contributing factor in today's retail stores.

Hopefully, you are now interested in becoming a Mystery Shopper and earning some of the benefits of Mystery Shopping, including "Getting Paid to Shop" and being reimbursed for your required purchases.

Mystery Shopping is a legitimate way to make extra money!

If you want to find out more, keep on reading!

If shopping is a crime.
Arrest me!

Chapter Two:

What is Mystery Shopping?

In today's economic climate, customer service is all important. Customers simply will not tolerate bad service and are too busy to tolerate slow service. Nowadays, customers want it right, and they want it now! If the service and products are not to their satisfaction, the customers will simply go to another store immediately. Customer loyalty depends on customer satisfaction.

For retail outlets, consumer experience with the store staff is everything. When the workers are courteous, helpful and knowledgeable, they will make a lasting impression and create loyal, satisfied customers. It is often helpful to measure the quality of the services offered, as well as to evaluate staff sales skills and their knowledge of the products offered.

Mystery Shoppers visit designated retail establishments as an average customer and complete confidential reports relative to the store appearance, customer service, the staff's knowledge of the product, and sales skills. Another

GET PAID TO SHOP: GUIDE TO MYSTERY SHOPPING

objective of Mystery Shopping is to provide management with the opportunity to evaluate the effectiveness of current training and operational programs. Professional Mystery Shoppers get to test new products, monitor register transactions, check operations, observe a store's security procedures, evaluate the effectiveness of advertising and assess other marketing efforts.

As a "Mystery Shopper" you will pose as an anonymous first-time customer. You carefully follow the avenue of a shopper from entering the store to the final sales transaction as a normal customer. Your shopping experience may require you to order an assigned meal, investigate an assigned product, or request an assigned automotive service.

Mystery Shoppers need to be reliable, organized, observant, flexible, honest and factual, and good writers. Sometimes you will need a digital camera to take pictures, or a scanner to submit receipts.

"Mystery Shopping" is an enjoyable type of work in which you act as a first-time customer in order to acquire certain information for the particular company that assigned you.

Chapter 3:

Mystery Shopping Assignments

Every one of the "Mystery Shopping" jobs you perform will be a new and exciting experience. From this point on I will refer to these various mystery shopping jobs simply as "assignments".

When you hear the word "job", the first thing that comes to your mind is probably work, and "Getting Paid to Shop" is anything but work. It's fun. It can also be informative, rewarding, challenging, and an adventure.

What other opportunities can you think of where you get paid for doing something that you already like to do? Plus, you usually get reimbursed for the product or service that you pay for. Service your car for free, and pocket a fee for doing so! Eat in restaurants for free, and get paid to do a report on the experience! Stay at a hotel for free, and earn money for evaluating your stay!

It is the Ultimate Dream Job.

GET PAID TO SHOP: GUIDE TO MYSTERY SHOPPING

"Mystery Shopping" is not difficult. A mystery shopper needs to be neat in appearance, be a good observer, and be able to complete a detailed report in correct English. Usually a typical assignment begins with a Business Representative contacting you by email and offering you a mystery shop at a certain store or many stores.

(A list of some businesses which pay you to mystery shop are included in this manual. All that you have to do is contact them by registering, and let them know that you are available to shop in your local area.)

They will then contact you with regard to upcoming assignments, which are shown on their website. Most of these businesses will even send you regular emails listing the upcoming assignments in your area. You define "your area" by deciding how far you want to travel. Twenty-five miles? Fifty miles? You will not get extra money for travelling within your defined area, but may be offered extra for assignments outside your area.

Each assignment will give you a time frame for that assignment during which you must complete the report. They might also ask you if you have any friends or family working at the store being shopped, because they want your report to be totally unbiased. They may also ask you a few more questions to determine your suitability for the assignment.

They usually let you pick the time and day of the week that you would like to go on a particular assignment, just as long as it is within the time frame that they have allowed. Because of the flexibility that Mystery Shopping offers in scheduling your valuable time, it is an absolutely perfect way to make lots of extra cash and also get free "gifts". If you are busy on one day and cannot go on an assignment, that's fine. You decide when you get paid to shop! On a few occasions, you may be required to go on an assignment at a specified day or time of day. Or, you can arrange your day to complete several assignments. Work as little or as much as you like.

After you have accepted an assignment the business will send you a Shopping Report Form and specific instructions that you require for that particular assignment. The Shopping Form will have various questions for you to fill in after you have completed your assignment. Some are simple check-boxes, and others require a detailed description. The Shopping Report Forms that businesses send you are all spelled out in detail and you are always encouraged to call the business if you ever have any questions.

The "Shopping Form" is used to explain how you felt as a customer when you shopped at a particular store. A typical assignment at a retail store usually focuses on the performance of the salesperson who helped you. Most often you will be asked to report on how long it took the employee to greet you, how they served you, and if their service was satisfactory. You may be asked to comment on their knowledge of the product, their efforts to up-sell or accessorize, and their customer connection skills.

These forms are not complicated. They have easy questions like: Did the salesperson greet you when you walked into the store? Were the products all arranged neatly on the display racks? Were you thanked for your business?

At the end of most Shopping Forms is a space for you to write down a short summary of your entire assignment, from your arrival at the store to your departure. A few short paragraphs will tell your experiences when you went shopping.

NOTE:

Before you go on your assignment, be sure to read (or even print out) the Shopping Form and the Guidelines ahead of time. They will help to give you an idea of what you are to check for while shopping. This will make it much easier to remember what happened after you have left the store. You should never take your Shopping Form into a store location and fill it out inside. This will instantly identify you as a Mystery Shopper, and you will be disqualified and not paid for the assignment. Be sure to wait until you get into your car to write down some notes, or when you get back to your home. Then, fill out the form right away before you forget your shopping experience. Most firms require your forms and receipts be submitted by upload within twenty-four hours of your assignment completion.

Also, before driving to an assignment, make certain that you know exactly how to get to the store. Most of the time you will be getting paid to shop in your local area. You may, however, accept an assignment that's in another city, and if you are not familiar with it, Google the exact location. If you are required to shop at a precise time be sure to allow yourself plenty of time to arrive early.

In any given week, you may be sent to a variety of different stores: a department store, a bank, a hair salon, a flower shop, a garage and more. The opportunity to shop at a variety of stores is virtually unlimited! For each assignment that you accept, you will receive a new Shopping Form to fill out. Treat every one as a new experience, reading the form carefully before completing the assignment.

If you don't think you can fully remember your assignments until the time that you get home (to fill out your form), take some notes when you get back in your car. Note the names of the people you interacted with – salespeople, cashiers, managers. Ask for a business card if one is available.

Note the time you began and the time you completed the assignments while it is fresh in your mind. Later on that day you can fill out your Shopping Form while consulting your notes.

Any day is a
perfect day
for shoe
shopping.

GET PAID TO SHOP: GUIDE TO MYSTERY SHOPPING
Chapter Four:

Success Tips

1.   Read over your Shopping Form and set of Guidelines (instructions) carefully before you go to each new assignment. In particular, note the location of your assignment. Often there are several similar locations in the same area (banks, fast food restaurants) and you must go the one which you have been assigned.

2. When you are given a certain time frame in which your assignment must take place, be sure to arrive at that location on time. Always allow enough time to complete the assignment.

3. Fill out your Shopping Forms as completely as possible. Review your form before you turn it in, to double-check that you have filled it out completely and accurately.

4. Do not take young children along on assignments where they may become a distraction to you. Remember, you are working and getting paid for it. Always take your Mystery Shopping seriously and act professionally.

5.   While visiting a store, don't attempt to stand out from the crowd. Dress the same way that you think everyone else who will be shopping there will be dressed. Always act like another ordinary customer. Your goal is to experience a normal shopping visit at each store that you visit. Don't do anything out of the ordinary to call attention to yourself as you conduct business with a store's employees.

6.   You don't have to look for things that are wrong. Don't harass employees or give them a hard time, to get them upset. Mystery Shoppers are supposed to experience how the average customer is being treated in a store, not how rude people are dealt with.

7.   If you shop at the same store more than once, each time that you go back, act as if it is your first time as a customer. Otherwise the employees may catch on to the fact that you're a Mystery Shopper.

8.   When you are filling out your Shopping Form, try not to use negative words that are demeaning or have racial overtones when you are describing an employee. For instance, if you are writing down a particular race use: White, Black, Asian, Hispanic, Native American, etc. Be objective in your observations.

9. Always keep your "Shopping Report Forms" confidential. Don't show anyone, and certainly don't ever give or sell your form to a store's competition. Take pride in being a "Mystery Shopper" because what you do is extremely important. Feel good about yourself. Have respect for the businesses who pay you to shop and for the stores you shop at.

10. Don't act like an inspector, looking into, under, around and behind everything. Shop like you would normally.

11. Be neutral. Don't act overly friendly or unfriendly. Don't start up unnecessary conversations with salespeople. The less attention you draw to yourself the better you will be. Just try to fit in and be one of the crowd. Try to give the salesperson an opportunity to be friendly, but don't try to force it. Your Shopping Report Form should report how employees behave in normal selling situations, and you are to follow the scenario described in your assignment. You will be told what questions to ask, what product to research, and other parts of the assignment that you must perform.

12. Be sure to get supporting documentation that you are asked for in your guidelines, such as the receipt for a purchase, the business card of the sales associate, or even digital photos of product displays and tags. Then upload them on your sales report. Remember: no supporting

documentation means no pay. In addition, if your assignments are not done properly, the company may not give you any future assignments.

13. Once you are done, you cannot go back to ask salespersons their names. Be sure to take notes as soon as you return to the car on staff names, time of arrival and departure, or similar small details that are easy to forget.

14. Retain copies of your paperwork for several months, including any photos, receipts, business cards and estimates given.

15. Respond promptly to any requests by the mystery shopping provider company for more information.

Chapter Five:

Your Shopping Summary

While you are writing the summary of your assignment, try to mentally walk through the entire shopping experience as if you have just lived it, from your arrival (note the time!) to your departure. Write your report as if you were recounting the experience to a friend. Include any relevant details that stand out. For example, if you walked into the store and noticed that there was water on the floor because it had just been mopped, but there were no warning signs, write that down.

It is not necessary for you to write your summary like an English teacher. Use simple, easily understood language. Avoid using overly familiar terms like: "Man, my experience at Hank's Hardware was totally awesome! I got this rad tool kit." Instead, you might say: "My experience at Hanks Hardware was quite pleasant. The salespeople were genuinely friendly and I bought a very high quality tool kit at a very reasonable price."

Do not be overly brief. The assignment requires details.

GET PAID TO SHOP: GUIDE TO MYSTERY SHOPPING

If you fill out your form with many uncommon words, the business person who reviews it will have to spend time trying to evaluate what you mean rather than concentrating on what you are saying.

Be accurate and truthful. If you didn't like a salesperson's hairstyle, or the colour of their clothes, it is not necessary to include that in your form unless you felt that it was unprofessional. Write down only the facts, not your own personal preferences. You should include your opinions on service, product quality, and overall store cleanliness.

Remember to submit your completed report within the required time, usually within twenty-four hours.

Always keep copies of your documentation including your receipt, digital photos, and your completed report. Some companies require you to keep these for twelve months.

Set up a file directory on your computer for "Mystery Shopping" and save each job in that directory, with files properly named for easy identification and retrieval. Keep paper files in file folders, organized by date and company. Never use the "shoebox" approach to filing your paperwork.

It is all part of being a professional "Mystery Shopper".

Chapter Six:

Getting Paid as a Mystery Shopper

The service area of the economy has greatly increased, creating a large demand for Mystery Shoppers. When a business wants to assign Mystery Shoppers, they invariably seek a Market Research Firm to provide them. The businesses you will be in contact with in this "Mystery Shoppers Package" are mostly firms who have contracts with hundreds of stores across North America, and need shoppers in all areas of the continent, not just in big cities.

As a Mystery Shopper, you will work on a contract basis. This means that you are not their employee, but rather an independent Mystery Shopper. You will be held responsible for your own income taxes on your earnings and no deductions will be taken out of your paycheck. Most people like this, because it allows them to take advantage of numerous tax breaks. As an independent Mystery Shopper, you can take advantage of tax breaks involving the use of your home as a place of work and the use of your car. You can also deduct the costs of doing business, such as internet costs, gas / mileage costs.

Some companies like to pay by cheque on a regular basis, such as every two weeks. Others issue cheques at the end of the month for all assignments completed in the previous month.

Some companies like to do a direct deposit into your own bank account, but you have to provide each company with your bank account and all branch and routing numbers.

Others prefer to direct deposit your payments into a Paypal account. **This is the most convenient and probably the safest way to accept payments.** If you have never used Paypal, it is easy to set up an account using your email as your account name, and then link it to your bank account so that you can easily transfer money into your own chequing account.

You will have to research each company and follow their procedures to receive payments.

I have never had a problem getting paid for my assignments. Most companies allow you to verify your pending payments and pay schedule on their websites once you log in. Keep a master list of payments from all your income sources and check them off when received. Remember, no deductions are taken because you are an independent business person responsible for your own accounting.

GET PAID TO SHOP: GUIDE TO MYSTERY SHOPPING

Chapter Seven:

Making Money Mystery Shopping

Now that you know how to Mystery Shop, the most important question you might have is "How much money can I make?"

The average shopping fee is about $20 per assignment. This does not include mileage or any other expenses. You may work the hours that you wish and do the work whenever you prefer. You might want to shop at your local book store, visit a fast-food restaurant, and get your car repaired all in the same week, or even on the same day.

Average fees for "assignments" are as follows:

Short "assignments" last about five to ten minutes. They usually pay from $5 to $15. Some examples are:
> Telephone Enquiries
> Convenience Store / Lottery Sales Agents
> Newsstand
> Dry Cleaner
> Gas Station (gas purchase)

Video Rental Store
Ice Cream/Yogurt Shop
Cash Loan Outlets
Phone order for Pizza Delivery

Medium "assignments" last about ten to twenty minutes. They pay from $12 to $25. Some examples are:

Drug Store
Fast Food Restaurant
Supermarket / Grocery Store
Automotive Supply Store
Specialty Stores in a Mall
Cell Phone Shops
Apartment Rental Agents

Long "assignments" may last thirty minutes or longer. These assignments pay from $20 to $40. Some examples are:

Fancy Eat-In Restaurant
Car Dealership Sales (Test Drive)
Hotel / Travelling
Bowling Alley, Theme Park
Bank
Auto Service Station (for vehicle service)
Store Audits
University Entrance Testing Centers
Casual Trendy Clothing Stores

GET PAID TO SHOP: GUIDE TO MYSTERY SHOPPING

Of course, in addition to your fee for completing the assignment, you are usually reimbursed any money you spent to complete the mystery shop. This may, for example, include the cost of the gift card you were required to buy (about $5) or the large pizza (about $15) or the cost of your car repairs (up to $65). You have to pay up front, but you get it back in addition to your shopping payment.

Without Mystery Shoppers, stores can usually only get information from the customers who are at the far extremes of the satisfaction scale, which is not a totally accurate viewpoint. Either they hear from those who are extremely happy, or from those who are extremely unhappy. To get proper feedback from the majority of the customers, stores need people like you. If a store were to worry only about the extremely happy or unhappy customers, they would be missing out on trying to improve service for the people who make up the largest part of their customer base.

While it is very important for businesses to deal with those customers who are very unsatisfied and to thank those who are very satisfied, it is even more important that they try to improve upon the experience of the vast majority of their customer base who are somewhere in the middle of the satisfaction scale. The ones in the middle spend the most, simply because of their sheer numbers. There are more of them. Herein lies their biggest market for customer loyalty and increased sales.

Chapter Eight:

Some Businesses That Pay You to Shop

The following is a listing of several of the larger businesses who will pay people, just like you, to shop as Mystery Shoppers. Each one operates differently. If you would like to Mystery Shop for any of them, you can contact these businesses, usually by signing up on their website.

When you apply, be sure to demonstrate the skills you will be using in your new job. Write in full sentences with proper punctuation and good English. You may be asked to provide a sample report of a recent dining or other service experience. Be sure to use proper terms such as SA (sales associate) or CSA (customer service agent), and avoid inappropriate language. Write the narrative from beginning to end. Do not offer opinions, just facts.

Since each of these businesses are different, you cannot possibly expect to get the same amount of money for each assignment that you may go on. If you got paid $25 to shop for a half hour from one business, that does not mean that the next business will pay you that same amount. Some of these businesses will allow you to get additional free product or merchandise when you shop by reimbursing you for money that you spent to complete the assignment. That depends on which store you'll be shopping at and what terms you have agreed to, before you shop. If you have questions about an assignment that you are going on, please contact the business that assigned you the job.

Please keep in mind that Mystery Shopping is not a nine-to-five job. The assignments that you may go on will vary. On a given day you might get pay a bill, test drive a brand new vehicle, and buy a new pair of designer slacks. There also may be days or weeks that you do not have any shopping at all. It all depends on the availability of stores to shop at in your local area, and if you are willing to travel and what times you are available to shop. Don't get discouraged if you don't meet your financial goals the first week. Everything takes time. Stick with it and enjoy your Mystery Shopping experience!

List of Mystery Shopping Companies:

You should contact the following businesses to register for Mystery Shopping assignments. They will of course keep your profile on file until they need you.

Note: Most of these businesses operate nationwide, even in Canada. Merely because their corporate address is not near you, it doesn't mean that you can't shop for them in your local area.

Bestmark Inc.
5500 Feltl Road,Minnetonka MN 55343

Website to register: www.bestmark.com

Bestmark offers assignments in both Canada and the USA, including many automotive assignments where you are reimbursed for service work done on your vehicle (to a maximum amount) plus a generous fee for the assignment.

Mystery Shopping Canada

Website: www.mscreporting.com
www.mysteryshoppingcanada.com

Assignments are available all over North America. Even if you don't do any mystery shopping on this site, it is highly recommended that you complete their eleven short on-line training courses for a variety of mystery shopping scenarios. For example, they provide guidelines for cash stores, banks, automotive assignments and restaurants.

C.R.I. (Corporate Research International)
Route 9, Box 44~7, Kinderhook, NY 12106

GET PAID TO SHOP: GUIDE TO MYSTERY SHOPPING

Website to register: www.mysteryshops.com

C.S.S., Inc. (Customer Service Solutions)
P. O. Box 3307, Van Nuys, CA 91407-3307

Website: www.cssamerica.com

Intouch Insight Mystery Shoppers
400 March Road, Kanata ON K2K 3H4 Canada
Website to register:
www.serviceintelligence.com/jobs/mystery-shopper.html

This company does assignments for Petro-Canada, First Choice Haircutters, Loblaws, Beer store ID checks, and many more, many of which are in small towns.

Monterey Mystery Shopping
2560 Garden Road, Suite 105, Monterey CA

Website: www.montereymysteryshopping.com

Monterey Mystery Shopping is the premier mystery shopping site for the automotive industry. Assignments include test drives, shopping for cars and motorcycles, or accessories such as jackets. No purchase is necessary, but a full-length photo in casual business attire may be requested.

Jobslingers
Website: www.jobslingers.com

Jobslingers is a portal site that allows you to access a wide variety of mystery shopping jobs from many different companies. You need to click through to the company websites and register with the individual companies in order to accept their assignments.

Premier Service
www.premierserviceshopmetrics.com

Premier Service contracts for many companies in the U.S. and Canada including Petro-Canada, First Choice haircutters and many mobile phone shops.

Mystery Shoppers Providers Association

You can join this professional organization for $25 per year, which includes your *Introduction to Mystery Shopping* Certification Course. Learn about Mystery Shopping including information and assistance links. Search the job boards for assignments.

Website: www.mspa-na.org

Don't forget to check out Mystery Shopping Magazine!!

GET PAID TO SHOP: GUIDE TO MYSTERY SHOPPING

Website: www.mysteryshoppingmagazine.com

This is a blog with lots of articles on mystery shopping, lists of companies looking for mystery shoppers, and open job assignments. Check them out!

Of course, in this age of the information highway, you could also just go to Google Search and type "mystery shopping" into the search box. You'll find a lot of other possible sites to visit.

Remember that no company that uses the services of mystery shoppers will ever ask for a fee or any other payment for your registration, training or testing. Steer clear of any such companies.

If you wish pay a fee to join a professional organization such as the MSPA, that is different as it is your choice.

Chapter Nine:

Completing the Shopper Report Form

NOTE: This is a sample only. Each time you go on an assignment you will use a different form. Always read them completely to understand the information you will gather.

STORE NAME
ADDRESS / WEBSITE / PHONE NUMBER

Questions may include the following:

Was outside of store clean and free of clutter?
Were windows and doors sparkling clean?
Was lobby area neat and clean?
Were all employees professionally attired?
Were you acknowledged within 30 seconds?
Were products neat and well-stocked?
Did the salespeople:
        Greet you in a friendly manner?
        Appear knowledgeable?
        Thank you?

GET PAID TO SHOP: GUIDE TO MYSTERY SHOPPING

Identify your needs with qualifying questions?
Know their products well?

You will most likely be asked to scan or photograph the receipt, the sales associate's business card, or even a photograph of the sales display in the store including the tags on individual items. Then you will need to upload these jpg files using the file up-loader on the company survey page.

NOTE: Failure to provide the required scans or photos will result in non-payment for the assignment.

And finally, you will be asked to write a brief summary of your entire shopping experience.

Chapter Ten:

The Outline of an Assignment

1. You will apply on the website for an assignment. The business will approve your application and will give you a time frame in which you must shop, usually anytime during one week and during regular business hours. You choose when to complete the shop at your convenience.

You may be asked to write a short paragraph on why you should be assigned this shop. I usually mention my availability, my capability, and my past experience in completing assignments.

For example, "I am a retired professional and am available any time or day to complete this assignment. I can write detailed and factual reports to given a true picture of what the average customer experiences in this location. I have completed many assignments in the areas of retail, restaurants and financial."

2. Before the assignment, carefully read or print out the Guidelines for the job, and the Survey / Evaluation form that you will complete after the job. Be aware of any particular questions you need to ask, and the tasks you must complete.

GET PAID TO SHOP: GUIDE TO MYSTERY SHOPPING

On the day of your "assignment", take your paperwork with you and leave it in the car. Give yourself plenty of time to arrive at the store. Dress in the same way you think everyone else will be dressed.

3. Make a point of remembering the salespeople, their names and descriptions, and how they treated you. Check out how products are displayed, without being obvious.

4. Important! Don't look for things that are either wrong or right. Just look for things as they are.

5. Do not volunteer information about yourself. Wait until the sales associate asks open-ended questions to determine what your needs are in order to make relevant suggestions.

6. When you've finished your shopping, don't hang around and watch other customers. Return to your car or house.

7. Immediately after you get home, fill out your online Shopping Form while the experience is fresh in your mind. Do not offer opinions. Do not comment on the ethnicity or physical characteristics of the staff.

8. Return your Shopping Form and supporting documentation by computer upload to the provider.

9. Best of all... <u>Have fun getting paid to shop!</u>

Chapter Eleven:

How To Observe for Your Shopping Report

Every "Shopping Form" that you fill out will be different. Some will have questions. Some will have fill in the blanks. Most require a written summary of what happened on your assignment. The best way to write a summary, is to write it just like you experienced it. Pretend you are telling your story to a good friend. Your summary doesn't have to be more than a few paragraphs or one page long. You don't have to go into extreme detail. To make it easier for you, here are some of the more important things that you should take notice of, as you shop and then write about later in your summary.

OUTSIDE OF STORE

When you get to the location, as soon as you step out of your car and start walking towards the store, start to take notice and remember what you see. You'll want to check if the parking lot was cluttered with shopping carts. Was the entrance area and outside displays clean, free of clutter, and easily accessible? Was landscaping well groomed?

Were all lights in the sign working? Were the posters in the window straight and neatly put up?

Take the time to observe closely. Even if there are no specific questions about the outside of the store, you should make some comments in your summary.

THE ENTRANCE WAY

The next thing you see on a visit is the entrance to the building. Is the walkway clean and neat or is it littered with cigarette butts and other debris? What about the doors? Are they clean? Are the windows clean? Are carts and baskets available as soon as customers walk in? Do customers have access to the newest sales flyer at the entrance way? Are they greeted when they walk in?

INSIDE THE STORE

When you get inside of the store, take notice of the area right inside the door. What was your first impression? Observe the floor. Does it have dirt, spills or garbage on it? Are the first product displays seasonally appropriate? Is it attractive to look at?

Notice things as you go about your shopping but don't go out of your way looking at every single detail. Just act like an ordinary customer and "see" only the things that you would normally see.

GREETING

Most stores assign one of their employees the task of greeting each customer who walks through the door. They may greet you right as you enter the store or after you've browsed a while. When someone greets you, the greeting should be a friendly one with eye contact made and a genuine smile given. Notice how long it took for an associate to greet you, to approach you while shopping, and to assist you in your purchase.

SHOWROOM DISPLAY AREA

The showroom is just another term for the inside of the store. It's the entire area where products are displayed. It's where you shop. When observing the showroom display area, you might ask yourself: How are products displayed? What is the condition of the area? Is it clean or cluttered? Does it provide a comfortable atmosphere? Are the products easy to reach? Are prices easy to see?

SERVICE

When you're shopping at places such as department stores, clothing, shoe or jewelry stores, this is where service comes into play. Service is not only limited to getting help finding a product. It is the overall "treatment" you receive from all store staff while you are in the store.

For example: Were salespeople friendly and fast to wait on you, or did they waste time messing around with things not related to the sale? Did the person who waited on you make you feel as if they were glad you were there, or did you feel that your presence was viewed as an interruption of what they were doing? Did they explain how to use a product, or leave you to figure it out on your own? Was the overall atmosphere as well as each employee's performance professional? Service is a broad category and plays a vital part in the success a store has.

With so many stores offering similar products, the real difference between them is the service offered to the customer. Good service encourages customer satisfaction. This leads to customer loyalty, good word-of-mouth both on social media and around the water-cooler, and increased sales for the store.

THE PRODUCT

The reason customers go to a retail outlet in the first place is to avail themselves of the product or service marketed by that particular company. Therefore stores are going to be particularly interested in your satisfaction with the product or service you receive. They may want to know if the salesperson tried to "upsell" (sell you a more expensive product) or tried to accessorize your product with some "add-on" purchases.

In all cases, the best way to evaluate the product or service is to hold it up against what you, as a consumer, would normally expect. If it's within your expectations, then it is a satisfactory product or service. When it falls out of this area, to what degree does it fail to live up to your expectations? Where did it fail? Have facts, not opinions. Cite specific examples, behaviours, or product deficiencies in your report.

SPECIAL AREAS

Special areas in a store include places such as the dressing rooms and rest rooms. It's important to check out these areas, too, because they play a very large role in the quality of a customer's experience. As you check out these areas, don't do anything differently than if you weren't a Mystery Shopper. For instance, don't ask the salesperson if you can go and look in the fitting room. Make sure you actually try a garment on. In the fitting rooms, notice if they are clean. Is an attendant handy? Are you limited to a certain number of garments at one time? What do you do with unwanted items?

The rest room is an area of real importance. Is it clean? Are hand soap, tissue and a hand dryer or towels available? Is there an employee form that is initialled every hour by an attendant?

CASH REGISTER

Of course, this is where the sales transaction takes place. While you are waiting for your purchase to be rung up, look to see how many people are waiting in line. Did the salesperson ring you up correctly or did they make a mistake? Did you get thanked for your purchase? Did you leave with a good impression and a feeling that you would like to return again to do some shopping?

Were there "impulse items" near the cash? These are inexpensive items such as chocolate bars, clearance merchandise, or magazines that shoppers pick up at the last moment without even thinking. Were they well-displayed?

LEAVING THE STORE

As you leave the store, make some final observations. Is the buggy or basket return area properly managed? Is the exit easy to negotiate? Do employees carry out bulky items for customers, or allow pick up at the loading area? Was there someone in the lot collecting buggies?

Chapter Twelve:

Mystery Shopping Quick Start Guide

Here is a "Quick-Start" plan to get you started making money as fast as you can. Follow this plan and you can be making piles of money in less time than you think!

1.   Read this entire manual, *How to Get Paid to Shop*. Even though you may be anxious to get started, you must first learn all you can about Mystery Shopping. If you miss something, in the long-run it may cost you an assignment.

2. Register online with one or more of the Businesses who pay people to shop as Mystery Shoppers. Don't feel like you have to register with all of the businesses at once. It's best to take it one step at a time to see if this is really something you like to do.

3. While you're waiting to hear back from a Business about your approval, read this manual again. The more familiar you are with "Mystery Shopping", the better you will do. Familiarize yourself with the company policies and training courses by moving around on their website.

4. Have someone take a photograph of you. Some Businesses will ask for your photograph, to put with your Application they keep on file. A head shot is fine. You certainly don't have to get a professional photographer. Just use any digital camera or the camera in your phone. Save the picture on your computer ready to upload. Scan your government identification (driver's licence) in case you are asked for proof of age (for test drives or beer shops).

5. Remember to be patient. Success will come your way if you do what it takes.

6. Keep track of your "Mystery Shopping" assignments, keep a computer file folder for your documentation, and keep track of your payments pending and received. If you are properly organized right from the beginning, you will have no problem handling a variety of assignments from a number of companies.

7. Be a professional. Complete assignments by the deadlines, and submit reports within the required time frame. Don't complain – just report the facts.

8. Prepare: compose several short paragraphs (100 words) on examples of good service and / or poor service, and why you should be selected as a mystery shopper. Save, cut and paste.

GET PAID TO SHOP: GUIDE TO MYSTERY SHOPPING
Chapter Thirteen:

How I Earned $1407.39 In One Month Shopping

(Reprinted from www.MysteryShopperMagazine.com)

"As a mystery shopper my life is different from day to day, week to week, and month to month. I mystery shop as my full-time job and it is my only source of income. In the month of April, 2016 I earned $1439.07 in shopper fees including bonuses and another $165.85 in useful reimbursements.

I started mystery shopping over eight years ago. What was only a few shops back then, has now become many shops each month.

Why? First, I liked it and realized it could become profitable and become my regular job. Second, I became disabled. I found it is a way to be able to support myself without going on full disability.

I shop five to six days a week usually taking Sunday off, except every now and then when I take one or two easy Sunday shops. I typically do my shops from 2 PM to 10 PM and reports anywhere from 10 PM to 4 AM. This is not straight time shopping or doing reports – it is just the time range when they are done and reported.

How did I make this much money in April? First let me start with the types of shops I performed. I did the following shops:

- Microsoft shops at both Microsoft stores and Best Buy Stores,
- Oil Change shops,
- Gas shops,
- Shoe shops,
- Fitness Center shops,
- Party Store shops,
- Bowling shops,
- Bar shops,
- Drug Store shops,
- Bank shops,
- Car and motorcycle shops,
- Movie shops,
- Hardware Store shops,
- Cell Phone shops,
- Highway travel centre shops,
- specialty retail shops,
- and, of course, lots of restaurant shops.

I am registered with over two hundred mystery shopping providers. I get my shops through emails and contact with schedulers. I look on job boards for individual mystery shopping providers (MSPs) or multiple MSPs, such as